WHAT'S THIS
I HEAR ABOUT
OUR CHURCH?

WHAT'S THIS I HEAR ABOUT OUR CHURCH?

An Action Guide for Congregation Leaders

Charles S. Mueller

AUGSBURG PUBLISHING HOUSE
MINNEAPOLIS, MINNESOTA

WHAT'S THIS I HEAR ABOUT OUR CHURCH?

This book is one of a series of paperbacks based on *A Study of
Generations*, a research project funded by Lutheran Brotherhood,
a Fraternal Benefit Society.

Manufactured in the United States of America

CONTENTS

Preface

Who needs an action guide? Pastors? Congregational leaders? Aren't they active enough? Many would say congregational leaders and pastors are far too busy to pause for studying anything other than those "necessary" things like reports, balance sheets, proven programs, and new projects. Who could want—or expect —more?

Yes, they are active, but activity is not enough. Far too often activity is little more than aimless busy-ness. There must be time to step back, take a look, and think. I suggest that slowing down may be just what's needed to make all those other "necessary" things really useful. The slowing down process is not intended as an acceptable way for getting a well deserved rest. Not at all. My hope is that this potential pause-that-re-freshes will give you a better understanding of your task, a new insight into your parish, and some of the information you need to make useful interpretations and effective decisions. As an elected official, an appointed committee member, or a professional staff person, you deserve that kind of help. But, before we get into that, let me share with you a series of experiences that prompted the preparation of this book.

I am a district president in my church body, responsible for the well-being of about 180 congregations, 60,000 congregational members, 200 clergymen, and as many Christian school teachers. As a district president I visit churches, one of the very pleasant tasks that falls to this position. Usually the churches I visit have a pastor's office. And just as usually, within that office, is a library to which the clergyman turns for help, the books that offer the help he feels he needs. Right in the middle of that library is usually one big, red book, *A Study of Generations*. It is the result of the most thorough investigation of any Christian denomination ever tried. The book's focus is on the Lutheran church bodies in North America. Packed into the pages of that wonderful book are a multitude of insights that can immediately help the most harried pastor, or the most agenda-ridden church council. In fact, paying attention to some of the things *A Study of Generations* tells us would immediately free up hours of the busy pastor's time (while taking the edge off many of his frustrations), and give a remarkable preciseness and purpose to any church council's activity.

But, like many things, its strength is its weakness. It's so big, and so filled with ideas, that some who need it most find they can't get started. It contains so much useful information that even the best of intentions fade away about page 40. I don't say this as a criticism of the authors! Our debt of gratitude to them is beyond expression. The scope of their project was remarkably ambitious. Anything less than a volume of the size they produced would not qualify as an adequate first-report of what they discovered.

But we do need a way to come to some of their findings in a manner better suited to the average among us. This little book is a part of a larger effort to place the value of their study at your disposal. It is offered as an aid for hard-working pastors and equally hard-working church councils.

As you prepare to use this book, I have a few comments to help you get started right. First, this book will make you work. It will require that you take a good close look at your congregation, and if you haven't done so already, it will require that you develop various maps, graphs, and charts to aid you in the study.

Second, this book is not intended to give quick answers. It is prepared to make you think. You will find that it is peppered with questions. I hope you skip none of them. If, for a moment, you slide past one or two, note them. Then, later, go back and satisfy yourself as to a proper response. You should also discover that I haven't exhausted the questions possible. Prepare your own and push yourselves for a usable resolution of them.

Third, this book is intended to be read by pastors, church council members, and committee members, individually. Then, *after* the private reading, it should be used as a discussion guide for the gathered group.

Discipline yourself to set aside the first 40 minutes of your council meetings, for the next year, as a time for working through this book. I can assure you that this will help you make quicker, better, and more confident decisions throughout the year.

For some of you the content of this book touches matters which are truly matters of life-and-death. No, not for you, personally, but for that congregation you love dearly enough to serve, either as its pastor or as a member of the group that will chart its future. For others this book will respond to your hope for more effective service. No one wants to waste time majoring in minors or proliferating piffle. Yet, tragically, that's about the level of activity at which many councils, boards, and committees operate. It's no wonder that a common church council complaint is the inability to enlist members of the congregation for service in various church offices! I suspect that these ecclesiastical conscientious objectors often have things pretty well figured out. Who wants to commit a major portion of time to a cause that offers little apparent hope for accomplishments. Is that judgment too harsh? Search your heart!

I visit 50 or more church council meetings a year, and have done so for the past decade. In addition, I've talked with thousands of church council members. If they weren't dedicated and loyal many would have bailed out long ago. Sadly, quite a few have!

Finally, this book is not a synopsis, but an attempt to give immediate application to some insights of *A Study of Generations*. I hope your appetite is whetted enough to make you want to dig into the study itself. I can assure you that it will be more than worth the effort!

Often as I have worked through *A Study of Generations* I have said to myself, "Wow! If I'd have known that 20 years ago!" Well, I know it now. For whatever years the Lord has yet reserved for my service to him and his people, the experience of working through the book will live with me and make me a much more sensitive pastor than I could ever have been without this experience. I now have the benefit of my labor and offer it to you.

To the authors — Merton Strommen, Milo Brekke, Arthur Johnson, Ralph Underwager—I am forever in debt for the vision and the effort *A Study of Generations* presents, and the ministry of love and assistance it is!

I have tried to weave some of my experiences in the manuscript. I disguised the specific place, the particular people, and individual events. While each event did take place, I don't want anyone to feel I was making fun. I'm as guilty as they! But, if we all can learn from others' mistakes, errors in judgment, or twisted thinking, we'll all be better for it, and the church will be so much stronger for it.

I owe thanks to many in the preparation of this manuscript. The pastors and congregations of the Southeastern District of The Lutheran Church–Missouri Synod who serve in a six-state area of the Eastern United States, regularly doing the impossible while setting the unusual as their average. Emma Hall, my dedicated co-worker and secretary, sees her service to all of us as a labor of love, generously given and competently performed. And, finally, I express my gratitude to the many congregations from coast to coast who have opened their meetings and the accumulation of their considerable wisdom to my view.

1

You Mean We Did Something Right?

I'll never forget the evening I spent at St. Paul's Lutheran Church. Those nice folks were lying in wait for me. They didn't intend to hurt me. They acted as they did because their parish pain was so intense that they needed someone on whom they might dump their load. And dump they did!

I was the newly elected district president coming to see how things were going in their family. My purpose was to gain some insight into their congregation and offer any assistance possible. In the course of the meeting, each member, in turn, felt compelled to tell me all the things that had been, were, and eventually would be wrong with their poor congregation. For more than an hour the unloading process went on. Each speaker strove valiantly, and usually successfully, to outdo the previous bearer-of-bad-news. It was grim. They had so much to tell! As each took his turn, the mood of the group steadily deteriorated. It got so bad that I'm sure if anyone had moved to disband the congregation, the vote would have been unanimous.

Finally, enough was enough! I broke into the chain of negative regurgitation with a simple request. I asked that the next five minutes of the meeting be reserved for those in the group who had something (anything!) positive to say. And, if no one would speak, we'd just sit in silence.

Those rather bedraggled brothers and sisters in Christ weren't quite sure what to do with that suggestion. It had obviously been quite a while since anyone in their group had spoken positively—or felt cause to. For the first minute or two the group bedded down in puzzled silence. Finally one man rose to speak. "You know," he said, "the ushering last Christmas Eve wasn't too bad!" At that a little laughter tiptoed through the group. Before long more voices were being raised on behalf of things that had gone right with the parish. That was a beginning. The corner was turned. I'm happy to report that now their congregation is doing OK. A number of changes took place (not the least of which was a change in their attitude). Today St. Paul's Church is alive and well and looking expectantly toward its future.

The mood of that first evening at St. Paul's is common in many churches today. There's a reason this is true. It's much easier for any group to testify to the negative things in congregational living than the positive. It's not that there are so many more negatives than positives, but being negative is safer. No one gets mad at you if you forecast doom and it doesn't happen. But if you speak positively, paint a rosy picture, dare to trust in the promise of tomorrow, and your prophecies turn out wrong, few people forget.

You are about to become a student of a potentially positive book called *A Study of Generations*. Almost all the insights of this book could be expressed either positively or negatively. For example: Chapter 5 of *A Study of Generations* shows that 40% of all Lutherans seem to misunderstand the gospel. That's a frightening thing! It sounds negative, for it could mean that after all our work—our Sunday schools, confirmation classes, Christ-centered preaching, Bible discussion groups, living in a Christian family—two out of every five Lutherans haven't gotten the message! Or so it would appear. But turn the coin over. State it positively. Isn't it remarkable that three out of every five Lutherans, or 60% of our total Lutheran family, have gotten the message! Isn't it fantastic that 60% rejoice in the truth of what God has done for us in Christ Jesus and seem to know how to flesh out this conviction in their daily life?

If you really want to press that insight ask yourself, "How many Lutherans comprehended the gospel 10 years ago? Or 20? Or 50?" While no proof can be marshalled to match that of *A Study of Generations,* there certainly are many clues. Read old sermon books and note the tone they communicated. Study the Sunday school material you worked with each week as a child. Check the old records of congregational meetings to define the past attitude of your parish. Compare the budget of the congregation in 1945 with one of 1965. How you spent your money says a lot! I believe a comparative evaluating would support the contention that today's Lutheran Christian has a more precise comprehension of the gospel's meaning than was true in some parts of our past. The point: we must expend as much effort viewing things positively as we naturally develop in support of the negative. Let's try it once.

A Study of Generations

A Study of Generations says that three out of five Lutherans are not actively involved in sharing their faith with others. It's important to know that. But the sentence isn't complete until we've noted that two out of five *are* actively involved in personally spreading the Good News in Christ Jesus. See how lifting up the positive changes our view? Let's try one more. If our study of Lutheran families suggests that brothers and sisters aren't very influential on each other (and that seems true within all age segments), let's recognize that and see what can be done about it. At the same time, do not overlook the fact that mothers are shown as highly influential in every congregation. With that knowledge we can reshape our congregational support emphasis. And from that knowledge comes our positive to match the previous negative.

Paging through *A Study of Generations* you will notice that the authors have very carefully written their report to keep the positive/negative aspects in useful tension. Yet, I am intrigued that so much of what has been written about *A Study of Generations* has emphasized the negative without recognizing the many positive things reported in the book. *A Study of Generations* clearly shows that many things are remarkably right in the church. No matter what the percentage of those who hold any given negative attitude, not one negative attitude in the church is unanimously held.

Further, there is no non-Lutheran theological posture that has captured the church. In the Lutheran church, at the very least, a sizeable segment holds to positive Christian attitudes, beliefs, and convictions and this group has not bowed the knee to any twentieth-century Baals, no matter what their shape. Granted, Satan has influence in the Lutheran church. But let it also be said that Jesus Christ is still the Lord of this church. The ultimate victor in the continuing struggle between those two has already been determined. Through the cross, and by the open tomb, Christ has overcome. The reality of that conquest is not a matter of whether! It is only a matter of when his reign will be apparent to all.

Say it! A lot of good things have been happening in and through churches for a long time! *A Study of Generations* will help you identify some of them in your congregation. So, let's turn there. How are things in your parish?

Back Home

It would be easy to lift up the negative things that have taken place in your congregation for the last generation, the last decade, or the last year. Church councils and pastors don't spend too much time talking about things that are going right, do they? It's those nagging negatives—not enough church attenders, not enough money, not enough teachers, not enough equipment, not enough classrooms, not enough chalk, not enough altar guild members, not enough pledges, not enough ushers, not enough choir members, not enough youth sponsors, not enough . . . . Is that the focus of your congregational discussion? Do you spend most of your time talking about things that aren't right, or aren't like they used to be, or aren't the way you'd like to have them be?

That kind of discussion is important, but to keep such comments from dominating, how about making the effort to *actively seek the positive?* Once you've tried it, you'll find it's not very difficult. You may even enjoy it. To get us moving in the positive direction, complete this sentence:

1. The thing I like best about my congregation is . . .

Now, in case there are some *advanced positive thinkers,* try this completion:

2. The *things* I like best about my congregation are . . . .

Now we have things moving. While you're in the mood, why not complete a few more sentences.

3. If there's one thing our congregation can be proud of (or, does well), it's . . . .

We can finish this little exercise in identifying the positive by completing the following sentences. Pastors are asked to complete 4(a), and laymen are asked to complete 4(b).

4a. I like the people of this congregation because . . . .

4b. I like my pastor and what he does because . . . .

As I write I wonder how many pastors and church council members will try to skip those questions. Visiting from parish to parish I notice a strange reluctance on the part of pastors and parishioners to state the obvious—if it's positive. It's not that they don't feel positive toward one another, but that they are unaccustomed to saying how positively they do feel.

Pastor, if your members show a loyalty to you even when you think they don't comprehend what you are saying (and maybe that's because you aren't speaking very clearly), why not thank them for their support rather than grumble about their ignorance?

And laymen, if your pastor is working hard to make his sermons more stimulating, can't you compliment him on the effort even though you may feel considerable improvement is still in order?

At one time I was in a group of pastors who agreed to visit congregations to encourage evangelism. We assumed that our visits would be generally quite painful since efforts toward evangelism usually are relatively modest. We agreed that we would not leave a parish without saying something positive about what they were doing. That wasn't an easy decision to make. As we anticipated the calls, we actually debated whether we should tell lies when nothing good could be said about what a congregation was doing! Moral conviction notwithstanding, we finally concluded that we would.

What fools we were! Once we committed ourselves to look for something good in the parish, we were amazed at the many obvious examples of real effort and accomplishment. None of our visitation teams found a parish so forlorn that nothing genuinely good could be said about it, or a pastor so inept that his only product was failure. We did find parishes that thought they were totally ineffective, and pastors who were convinced that they were absolutely inept. Satan will always headline your failures. Christians should be just as active in re-enforcing the positive about one another. Even more so!

The Church Council Meeting

Up to now we have been focusing on what you can do individually, prior to the meeting. That church council meeting is coming. Others in your group have (or should have) read this same chapter, and hopefully will have completed those earlier sentences. Insist that your council talk about all those sentences. For a moment leave the cracked windowpanes in the basement alone. Forget about the building-fund balance—it's not that much anyway. Ignore the parking problem that has preoccupied you for the last three meetings. Make some time on your agenda for sharing the positives of your life together. If you haven't a better idea for an agenda, try this:

1. Let all read their completed sentences. Don't wince! Don't correct! Don't debate! Just let those sentences be heard in your council and flow across your Christian consciousness. Maybe, on another occasion, you'll want to hear more from one or the other who has completed the sentence in a most tantalizing way. For the moment just let the sentences hang in the air.

2. If you have a written agenda, look it over. How much is negative? Can negative things be stated in positive terms? *(For example:* If the financial report reads, "67 out of 98 family units of our congregation are at least $100 in arrears of their pledges for the year," can that information honestly be cast positively? Is there a positive dimension to it? Which is more amazing, that 67 families are in arrears, or that 31 families have been led to meet their pledge completely?)

3. While you are at it, having stated things positively, how do you drop the other shoe? We don't want to ignore the areas of our congregational life which need correction or improvement, but there are ways of stating these things that actually get at the correction and the improvement. Does your group have the potential for that kind of creative, positive Christian work?

4. If you have no agenda for this meeting, read through the minutes of your last meeting. Lift out the negatives and see how much time you spent focusing on what wasn't going right.

Of course, there is more to facing opportunities and challenges that confront the church than stating things positively. Failure *is* failure; sin *is* sin; painful truth *is* painful truth. The authors of *A Study of Generations* make that clear. They do not gloss over problems confronting the church or ignore brutal facts. At the same time they are aware, as each of us should be aware, that grace *is* grace; victory *is* victory; redemption *is* redemption; forgiveness *is* forgiveness; hope *is* hope; a better way *is* a better way. You can never understand the situation you are confronting unless you can see both the positive and the negative—and have them in a proper and balanced perspective. While you're probably not where you want to be, you're better off than you had ever thought! Getting the most out of *A Study of Generations* means you must have a clear picture of your parish and a clear understanding of the church which, by the grace of God, has done many things right.

2

Who's Who
in the Pew?

William F. Bruening, pastor for many years at Christ
Lutheran Church in Washington, D.C., annually led
his congregation through a ritual called, "Who's Who
in the Pew?" While his scope of interest was limited,
the intent of his effort is worth noting.

Christ Church served people from all over the
United States, people who became members during
their tour of duty in the capital. That Sunday when the
ritual was practiced included a roll call of states. It
began with Alabama and ended with Wyoming. He
used the result of this roll call to gain understanding
of the people in his parish so that he might better
serve them. He also wanted to give his members a
little better insight into each other so that there might
be fewer misunderstandings and a deeper sense of
fellowship. In this, and by using many other sensitive
pastoral techniques, he was ahead of his time. Instead

of assuming that he already knew all there was to know about the people he served, he was always ready to discover and share a new insight about the parish.

Most pastors with whom I talk really believe they "know" their members. Clergymen have a way of confidently claiming complete insight of their congregational condition by stating, when a new suggestion is made, "Now, in my church, the people feel that . . . ." or "People at Trinity would never buy that idea," or "My congregation has always taken a position that . . . ." That's the way it is with pastors. Many think they know their congregation in the same way a doctor knows exactly where the appendix is. But there is more than enough evidence to suggest that this pastoral insight is not as complete or as infallible as some pastors would like to think. Unlike their medical friends, pastors can't bury their mistakes! Their errors hang around to hound them for years.

Happily (or unhappily) pastors don't have the corner on the infallibility market. Has anyone at your church council meetings ever spurned a new suggestion saying, "That won't work. I've already had a number of phone calls about it and I know that the people here feel . . . ." or "I've been a member of this congregation for 13 years and I can tell you that our people will never . . . ." Some congregational officers, too, think they have their finger right on the pulse of the parish. Since pastors change more often than that hardy, central-core of congregational leadership, the council members may feel they have a better and more precise understanding of the will of the parish than even their pastors—and be just as wrong!

If you attend conferences at the regional or national

level, you soon see that it works the same way. "The people of Iowa have always felt that . . . . " or "The Lutheran Church in America has a history that would never permit . . . . " It isn't necessary to list the specifics for these imaginary quotes. Let the subject be theology, or race relations, or a new stewardship plan, or a program of social action, or the church-dabbling-in-politics, and people are convinced that they "know."

The amazing thing about this is that most actually know very little. With a modest amount of substantiating evidence many leaders seem capable of extending unsupported generalizations into eternal truth! We all have the tendency to take a single experience and embroider it until it becomes the seed for an insensitive (and often irrelevant) ecclesiastical generalization applicable to the local, regional, or national level.

Your congregation may be different from all other congregations. A Study of Generations quite clearly states that variations within congregations, and between congregations, are less extensive and thus more predictable, regardless of the synod, and regardless of the national region, than anyone to this time has suggested.

Take a few moments to find out if that's true. Who's-who-in-your-pew? Or if you use chairs, "Who's-there-in-our-chair?" Let's try to get a better picture of who you are, and then develop that picture within the context of our brothers and sisters across the nation. For starters, check the following items selected from A Study of Generations and see how they match your congregation. These, plus additional information you ought to have about your group, can set the stage for a discussion that might affect your style of ministry.

1. *A Study of Generations* **says that Lutheran congregations are overwhelmingly white congregations.** Is yours? One thing is certain, that isn't the case with our nation. And it most certainly is not the reality of our world.

What's your estimate about the racial makeup of your community _____; your state _____; the nation _____? I could give you the answers to those questions, but searching them out for yourself is a most useful way of growing in understanding. The information is really quite easy to find. It's all in the 1970 census data, readily available in every community, for every community.

But what difference does it make if you have a predominantly white congregation? Does a congregation think or act differently if its membership is 98% (or 85%, or 43%) white? Will some useful ingredient be missing if this is true? Would you believe that people of another racial grouping may have an insight into the mission of the church, or into our opportunity of service, which is difficult for a white person to perceive? Could it be that we have grievous misunderstandings of those we do not know, except as racial caricatures? Could it be that "they" have much to teach us, and that without their instruction we are only partially educated?

Those are a few of the questions that press forward when we talk about the racial makeup of any congregation. In discussing these questions various apprehensions, fears, and misunderstandings will certainly surface. They also bring with them the possibility for effective congregational life and full commitment to the Christ-life.

2. **Women make up a large percentage of our membership.**

This is no women's-lib insight. One national Lutheran body has a female membership of 60%. It's a *Christian-lib* concern. The number of women in your church will force any church council to ask serious questions of themselves and of their congregational style. What *is* the role of women in your parish? What has it been in the past? In what way have women influenced the direction of your congregation? How can their potential for greater effectiveness be stimulated? The day for limiting women to the Ladies' Aid is long past. Your church council must recognize this!

A Study of Generations has so many things to tell us about the role of women in the church that glossing over this area of inquiry would be most foolish. It is time for each congregation to evaluate the role of women in its work.

3. *A Study of Generations* **says that most members of the Lutheran church are now native born, and most members over 50 years of age have a North European background.**

The language battle of 50 or more years ago, probably the most traumatic struggle our churches have faced to date, is over in all but a few of our congregations. The joke told today in Swedish, Norwegian, German, or Slovak, will be understood by only a handful in any parish. The language question may be solved, but a more pertinent concern for today is the mind-set that permeates our congregations derived from our Swedish, Norwegian, Finnish, German, or other North European heritage.

Only 3% of today's Lutherans between the ages of 15 and 18 have foreign-born fathers. The figure jumps to 28% for Lutherans between the ages of 50 and 65. And if one were to ask how many members have foreign-born grandfathers, the percentage would take another leap. But think about our hymns, our orders of service, the structure of our congregations, our parish practices. Many of these were transplanted from North European church life to North America, and still flourish, translated but essentially unchanged, after more than a century. How does the non-North-European Lutheran of the 1970s relate to all this? Do any traditional practices in our congregations actually keep people out? Are there practices and traditions we ought to include so that we may more effectively serve?

4. *A Study of Generations* **tells us that we are about evenly divided between white-collar and blue-collar membership in our church.**

That wasn't so even a generation ago. Lutherans were then what sociologists called the blue-collar working class. The attitude and values of workmen, craftsmen, and non-managerial people shaped the way our congregations related to authority, to standards of conduct, to materialism, and to order in the church. More than that, being blue-collar in the 1970s means something different from being blue-collar in the 1930s. Each of us is most certainly our father's son, but we aren't our father. We are significantly different from our father. Do you agree? If so, in what way are we different? In what way are we the same? Does the blue-collar/white-collar division of your congregation, or of your community, affect what your congregation thinks, how it acts, and what it can reasonably expect to accomplish?

5. *A Study of Generations* **discovered that Lutherans are above average in their level of educational achievement.**

Why do Lutherans have such a lofty view of the value of education? Is there something in our institutional makeup, or in our theology, which suggests that education is very important and usually worthwhile? Does the national Lutheran average of one-third of the congregational membership having at least some college education affect the kind of congregational educational programming, the preaching, or the practice of the life in Christ which is possible and desired in your church? Is there a difference in worship attendance, involvement, or committed activity in your parish between those who have had some college education and those who have not? What about the commitment to education in the future of your parish? Will there be more, or less, or about the same number going to college? Will this make any difference in your congregational style?

6. *A Study of Generations* **reports that more than three-fourths of our families have an annual income in excess of $9000.**

That figure is already somewhat outdated. Since 1970, income levels have further increased. By 1975 the correct figure would be $10,000, or perhaps even more. Translated into realities of congregational life, an income at that level means that our families are able to do things which a few years ago would have been economically impossible. They can actually buy a cabin on the lake or in the mountains. They can own a boat. They can afford longer vacations and take weekend jaunts. They can retire earlier. Our families are able to do so very many things that directly affect the congregation and its life, things impossible a few years ago. Affluence can be a liability that may affect your congregation's vitality.

But there is a positive side. More income means our membership can increase their commitment to the mission of the church. They can underwrite larger and more ambitious efforts to share the gospel with others and more vigorously respond to the needs of the have-nots of this world. But how do your people see this wealth? Are they willing to acknowledge their wealth? Do they see it as something that can serve, or do they use it as something that is self-serving? What have you done to help them see their blessings properly? Please don't make any easy generalizations in this area. Take some time.

To help your discussion of this subject, ask each one to jot down on a piece of paper whether his annual income is more or less than $10,000 per year. And then ask each to estimate whether the congregation is basically above or below the $10,000 level of annual income per family. What are the problems of those who make less than $10,000 a year? And what problems does a person have who makes more than $10,000 per year? Talk for a few moments about money and its effect on all of us and its potential for good or for evil within the congregation.

7. *A Study of Generations* **says that 20% of our members have had a serious home difficulty in the past year.**

That's really quite a figure. Even those who did the work on *A Study of Generations* were modestly amazed at this result. In breaking the figure down, they determined that with the exception of those in the age group 24 to 29, every other group exceeded the 20% figure for serious home difficulty within the past year. In the age group of 42 to 49, the figure reaches 25%. "Home difficulties," while not specifically defined, do *not* include those who have been ill, or were hospitalized, or who needed counseling for emotional problems, or who were on welfare. That's another category of people in our parish!

To fill out this part of your picture of parish need, 5% to 10% of each age group did seek counsel for emotional problems during this past year; 3% to 5% were on welfare; 4% to 11% have been frequently ill during the year; and 9% to 25%, depending on the age group, experienced hospitalization.

What a reminder to us of the internal need for ministry! What a message for any pastor as he prepares his sermon. Those people out there in the pew are not placid individuals with few daily difficulties. Quite the contrary. They have faced, and are facing, serious problems in a variety of areas. This is a constant reality.

How well would those percentage figures match your parish? Do you know? And what do these figures say to the style of pastoral and supportive ministry your parish practices? Could some delinquency have developed because no one sensed, and then responded, to real need?

8. *A Study of Generations* **informs us that while we marry within the Lutheran family, most of our closest friends are outside of our congregation.**

Does that startle you? In response to the question, "How many of your five closest friends are members of your congregation?" the following scale was developed:

Age Group	15-18	19-23	24-29	30-41	42-49	50-65
3 or more	17%	14%	15%	24%	30%	43%
2	19%	14%	16%	19%	19%	16%
1	23%	23%	15%	17%	15%	12%
0	41%	49%	54%	50%	37%	29%

Think about that. There could be so many interpretations of those figures. Are they good or bad for your congregation? Good or bad, the scale has much to say about the kind of relationship we have with one another. The scale also offers some answers to problems that worry us about commitment, church attendance, participation in congregational get-togethers, and other activities that don't seem to work out too well. When 49% of our members between the ages 19 and 23 have none of their five closest friends in the congregation (and in the age group 24 to 29, 54% have none of their five closest friends as members in the congregation), we have a problem. Or is it an opportunity?

Paralleling these figures on friendship is another most interesting one. We marry Lutherans! Seventy-three percent of all Lutherans report that there are no non-Lutherans within their immediate family, and an additional 16% report only one or two. Though recent national trends suggest that there are more intermarriages between members of different religious bodies now than in the past, that does not seem to be true for Lutherans. One possible explanation is that Lutherans marry non-Lutherans and then convert their marriage partner to this religious affiliation. Test that out in your congregation.

9. *A Study of Generations* **shows that nearly 75%
   of all Lutherans have been a member of their present congregation for five years or more.**

It looks like once we join a given congregation we stick. We may move our area of residency, but we don't move our church membership. Is this kind of membership a plus or a minus? Does it mean that people are really living farther and farther away from the church building but are still keeping their membership in the parish? Check out the mobility pattern of your congregation. Have they been moving? What effect does where your members live have on your congregational activities? What effect does it have on their level of participation?

10. *A Study of Generations* **says that 75% of our members feel they are religious, or more religious than their parents.**

That may say something about the level of present religious commitment, or that of the past, or it may just be egotism! But, it could be a fact. Would you say that you are as religious, or more religious, than your mother and father? What difference does this insight have upon your congregational style of life?

When we couple this insight with the question asked by *A Study of Generations*, "What are the two greatest influences on what you are now?" an interesting picture develops. All age groups list their mother as the most influential force on what they are now. For those in the age group from 15 to 29, the second place of most influential is given to their father. As we grow older, the father's influence slips to third and fourth place. God begins in fourth place as most influential among the youngest, and moves up to second place among the oldest. Friends are placed in third place as most influential among the youngest, and drop sharply to nearly last place among the oldest. The church begins in sixth place among the youngest and climbs steadily to third place among the oldest. School, teachers, and other families remain rather low in the category of most influential, all across the age span. Of great interest is the fact that the category of "brothers and sisters" is in last place as most influential in all age groupings.

But think of it. If at least 40% to 50% of every age group believes their mother is the most influential force in their lives, and if between 25% and 40% list their father as the most influential force in their life, and if a total of 75% think they are *as* religious, or *more* religious than their parents, what a powerhouse of potential there is in the church!

Back to Us

These ten findings from *A Study of Generations* are illustrative of the kinds of information it contains. There are many other items, which, together, give us a better idea of the attitudes of church members. We could have added that Lutherans are concentrated in the Midwest, are not nearly as mobile as most Americans, are about evenly divided in the size of the community in which they are reared, are 40% Republican and 25% Democrat, 25% are in professional or managerial positions, less than 10% are farmers. All those things are crucial to a proper view of Lutherans. And there is so much more. As you can see, *A Study of Generations* knows a lot about Lutherans!

But, as much as *A Study of Generations* knows about Lutherans, you have the finest potential for discovering truth about your congregation. To get you going on how to use this chapter, divide the ten items cited in this chapter among the church council members. Ask each member to take one or more of the items and isolate its meaning for your congregation. One way to do this is by writing out answers to the questions which are included under each item. Answer every question as fully as you are able. Once you have given your best response, see if you can isolate additional information that would make for further completeness. And then write down questions which come to your mind as you work on these answers. Finally, put all the answers together in a notebook and give each member a copy. Then let every member have a chance to work through all the answers, giving them a chance to comment, correct, flesh out, or otherwise give their input. That will be an invaluable document for orienting new council members in the future and will also serve as a control base from which you can update the answers every few years. You'll never regret taking the time to do this. Your answers will help you right now, and future councils will honor your effort with better decisions, sharper planning, and deep gratitude.

3

See Yourself
As You Are

If you want to effectively use the information developed in *A Study of Generations*, you need a clear congregational portrait for comparison. If you don't have this comparative portrait, it won't be long before you'll be saying things like, "Well, all that stuff looks good enough, and probably applies to others, but it doesn't fit our situation."

Maybe it doesn't fit your situation. But before you reach that conclusion, you need to know what your situation really is. Developing a picture of yourself, as you really are, is not optional, no matter what you finally do with the results of *A Study of Generations*. Nor is it easy. It will require hard work. Generating the will to perform hard work is not the simplest thing in the world. To show you why the hard work ought to be done, answer the following questions on the basis of information which you already possess about your congregation and your community. Let all church council members do this without reference to any records and without additional research. After all have answered the questions, assign one member of the group the task of getting the accurate data. It will require checking your congregational records and address lists. Match your answers with those of others on the council and with the answers you got from your records. Here are the questions:

1. We have _____ souls in our congregational family.

2. We have _____ confirmed members in our congregational family.

3. We have _____ family units in our congregational family.

4. The median age of our congregation is _____.

5. _____% of our family units include both the mother and father.

6. There are _____ elementary-school children in our parish.

7. There are _____ junior-high school children in our parish.

8. There are _____ high-school children in our parish.

9. There are _____ college students in our parish.

10. There are _____ widows/widowers in our parish.

11. There are _____ retired people in our parish.

12. Most of our people travel at least _____ miles to come to church.

13. _____% of our total membership is female.

14. _____% of our membership has belonged to this parish at least 5 years.

15. _____ families have become a part of our parish in the past 5 years.

16. We have _____ non-white family units in our parish.

17. Our community is _____% non-white.

18. _____% of our membership under 40 years of age has gone to college.

19. Yes/No—Our church council is reflective of the congregational makeup in terms of age.

20. Yes/No—Our church council is reflective of the congregational membership in terms of how long they have belonged to this parish.

21. Yes/No—Our church council is reflective of the congregational membership in terms of sex distribution.

How did you do? These aren't all the questions that ought be asked (and for which you ought have accurate answers), but these relate directly to almost every decision your church council makes. To gain the most from *A study of Generations,* a pastor and his church council need to know hard facts about their parish. Without this factual information they will continue to operate with loose estimates. It's not difficult to gather accurate data, but it does require effort. Let me suggest a few simple tools you could develop to help you see yourself as you really are.

Population Pyramid

If I could have just one measuring device for developing a sharp picture of a congregation I would opt for a population pyramid. A population pyramid looks like this:

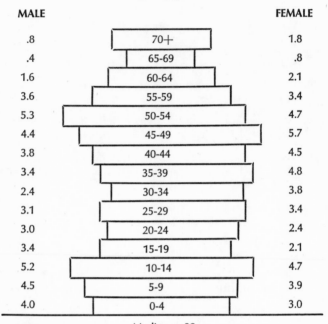

891 SOULS

MALE	Age	FEMALE
.8	70+	1.8
.4	65-69	.8
1.6	60-64	2.1
3.6	55-59	3.4
5.3	50-54	4.7
4.4	45-49	5.7
3.8	40-44	4.5
3.4	35-39	4.8
2.4	30-34	3.8
3.1	25-29	3.4
3.0	20-24	2.4
3.4	15-19	2.1
5.2	10-14	4.7
4.5	5-9	3.9
4.0	0-4	3.0

Median — 38

The easiest way to develop a population pyramid is to follow these steps:

1. Begin with two pieces of paper, marking one of them *male* and the other one *female*.

2. On the left side of the paper list the years, in five-year increments, in reverse order, beginning from the present year. (If this were 1970, your first set of figures on the upper left-hand corner would be 1970-1966, 1965-1961, 1960-1956 and continue in that way to the year 1901, so that your total list would span 70 years. The last figure you would place on the left-hand side would be "1900 and before.")

40

3. Take your congregational records. Read through them, or ask someone to read them aloud to you, from A to Z, lifting from each membership record the individual's sex and year of birth. As each name is mentioned make a mark in the proper year segment, on whichever of the two pages is appropriate. Unless your congregation is unusual, you will probably discover that not all the dates of birth are listed. Do not bypass these names. Guess their age as best you can. When you are finished with this part of your work, you will know how many males and how many females belong to your parish (and adding them together you will have the total number of souls in the congregation), and you will have the entire congregation divided into five-year age segments.

4. In your next step convert these individual numbers, by age segments and by sex, into percentages. If you have a total of 600 souls in your congregation and there are 42 females between the ages of 0-4 (that would mean they were born between 1966 and 1970), this converts to a figure of 7%. If you have, in the same age segment, 29 males, that figure converts to 4.83%. Round out the percentages to the nearest tenth. This may mean that your final total will be a bit less than 100%, or perhaps a bit more, but that degree of accuracy is sufficient. After you have completed that for each age segment, by sex, you are ready for the next step.

5. Using graph paper, convert your findings into a series of bar graphs. You do this by "stacking" the age divisions (0-4, 5-9, 10-14, 15-19, etc., to age 70. Make your last category, 70 plus.) And then fill in your per-

centages on the appropriate bar. Your pyramid should look something like the one in our illustration. But chances are the age bulges will be different. Maybe *very* different.

Now you are ready to study your results. If the bars are longest at the top, it means that you have many older people. Congregations with a top-heavy population pyramid had better not embark on long-range building programs without considerable interpretation of what these bulges mean. If the longest bars are in the area of the 50s, you can deduce that in a relatively few years a great many of your members will be ready for retirement. If the heaviest lines are in the earliest years, your church council will have to ask pointed questions about youth-related activities and whether you are truly ministering to young people.

A population pyramid should certainly be developed before any congregation decides to build new or additional facilities. The facilities you build should be related to the needs of your congregation. I've never forgotten the congregation that built a gymnasium, only to discover that their population pyramid showed there weren't that many youngsters in the congregation and fewer yet coming along.

As valuable as one population pyramid may be, the greatest value develops when you have prepared a population pyramid year-by-year for five or more years. By placing them side by side you can see how your congregation is changing and what changes you may reasonably expect for the future—unless something unusual takes place. After a while, you will become skilled at anticipating the changes and can use this anticipation for your future programming.

Your population pyramid will be even more useful if you construct a population pyramid for your community, or for the census tracts around your parish, using the 1970 census data. Match your congregational pyramid with that of your community. Are they similar? If they are different, in what ways are they different? What does your community population pyramid tell you about the potential for ministry in your area? What does your congregational population pyramid tell you about your potential for responding to the opportunities your community presents?

Pin Map

The second tool you could develop and update annually is a pin map. A pin map is just what its name implies. Place a good map of your community on soft material that will allow you to stick pins. Then place a pin at the address of every member of your congregation. If you use the numbered pins available through most office supply stores, you will find it much easier to keep your map up-to-date. Match the pin number to a member of your congregation, and if that member moves, the numbered pin may be moved as well.

And what does a pin map show you? It shows you where the members live. It also shows you where they don't live. If none of your members live near the church, don't be surprised if the parish leadership has trouble developing congregational interest for projects of community service! The distribution of your membership may be very directly related to the frequency, or the best time of day, or the response you may expect for church activities. Many well-conceived and valuable congregational efforts have failed because no one took the time to check where the people lived from whom the activity was planned!

Overlays

The next tool you need to develop is an overlay map. For this you will need a map of your community, some large sheets of clear plastic, and model-airplane paint of various colors. Place a sheet of clear plastic over the map, and then, using the paint, dot onto the map the places where people live when they joined your church. On the first sheet mark the place where people who were part of our parish lived ten years ago. Then, beginning with nine years ago, and using a different color for each year, dot three years of information (9, 8, and 7) on each sheet. On a third sheet do the same for years 6, 5, and 4. Continue this process until you are up-to-date. When all of this is done, go back over each sheet, and using red, or some other visible color, encircle any dot from which a member has moved. In that way you can visually determine the areas your members are leaving, and the areas from which members are joining.

Ask yourself questions like, "Are members moving away from the church building, or are they moving nearer?"; "From what areas of our community do we seem to get most of our members? Why?"; "Why do members join from one area—or another?"; "Why are there gaps on this map? Are there no homes in those areas, or have we failed to make an impact on part of our community? Why?" These and many other questions will force themselves forward for consideration, and hopefully for a useful answer.

Length of Membership

One final useful graph shows how long people have belonged to your parish. Check your records to determine when present members joined the congregation. After you have gathered the data, convert this information into a graph like this:

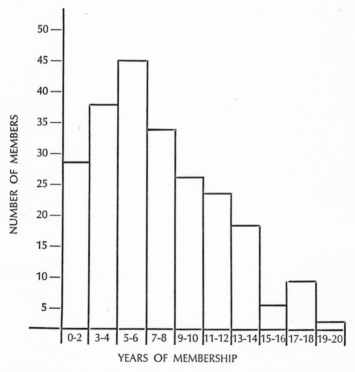

Now look at your congregational leadership — all those who serve in appointive, or elective, offices of the church, ranging from the church council, to Sunday school teachers, to officers of auxiliaries, to all others who would fit in categories like that. Make a length-of-membership graph about them. This graph will show you how long a person must be a member before he can expect to assume a leadership role. You may have a probationary period and not even know it. It also may show that only the newest members are willing to accept leadership responsibilities. Look it over carefully and see what you discover. Compare it with the full membership graph. What do you see?

Variations on these graphs are possible. You may wish to develop a graph showing male and female congregational leadership. Or you may wish to work up a graph showing how long young people remain members in the congregation from the time of their confirmation.

Depending on the congregation, the information you seek may be readily available—or next to impossible to procure. You may have to develop a simple questionnaire for distribution to your congregation. If you don't already have complete records, now is a good time to get them. With those records in hand you not only derive greater benefit from *A Study of Generations,* but you'll be better prepared for all the planning that is so crucial to your parish life. It's time to get it all together, and see yourself as you really are.

4

I Wonder How
They're Thinking—and Why

As a parish pastor I have often been surprised in congregational meetings by the way men and women conduct themselves. Some are marvelously consistent —they are *always* against anything new. Others lack that consistency. The same fellow who fought the painting of the gym last month makes the motion to redecorate the office this month! Such erratic behavior is often baffling to those who have been asked to lead. Another intriguing group includes those who will go along with anything just as long as no apparent changes are made. I still remember when we couldn't square-dance in church, but could play party games. (For those whose memory is limited, "party games" was what square dancing was called in churches that didn't allow square dancing!) Finally, there is that lovely person who brightens up whenever anything new is proposed —no matter what it might be.

Change or No-Change?

I was helped considerably in this grapple with quirks of Lutheran behavior when late one evening, at a retreat house in Connecticut, Ralph Underwager, one of the authors of *A Study of Generations,* drew a little box and scribbled some letters at the four corners. His box looked like this:

TC	TNC
SC	SNC

The *TC* stands for *transcendental change*. *Transcendentalism* is the term used to describe an understanding of life which recognizes there is a force at work outside ourselves. This force exerts itself in our life in ways we cannot understand but which we accept, and it inserts truths into our life which are not provable but which we believe. People who believe in a powerful and presently active God may be called transcendentalists. Believing in the loving power of a caring God, and trusting that he both can and will assist in all kinds of circumstances, is a type of transcendentalism. To be a *transcendental-change* person is to believe that God is in charge of the world, is powerful under all circumstances, and that he takes the threat out of what might be unknown. Transcendental-change people are not petrified when world history, or events in their life, take a sudden and even threatening turn. They believe that "all things work together for good to them that love God." With that conviction, they just wade in! Most of our forefathers volun-

48

tarily crossed the ocean to come to the new land, leaving all that was familiar behind. They were mostly transcendental-change people. Those who were pressured by other factors (war, persecution, poverty) *may* also have been, but those additional factors make it harder to tell. Most non-transcendental people stayed home—or soon returned.

The *TNC* stands for the term *transcendental no-change*. Springing from the same view of God as that held by the transcendental person, the *transcendental-no-change* person believes that while God is present and in charge of the world, he expects things to be left pretty much as they are. It is the responsibility of the transcendental no-change person to make sure that's what happens! Transcendental no-change people lean heavily on tradition, on history, and on things that have taken place before. Passing on to the next generation exactly what was passed on to theirs is very important to them. Any ancestors who came floating across the water with the characteristics of transcendental no-change were unquestionably in the minority. The TNC people who did come were perhaps motivated to do so by their attachment to others, by some pressure that made it very important that they leave the "old country," or perhaps in the mistaken notion that they could really build in the new land the same kind of life they had in the old country. Some of the early religious settlements in the United States were developed by transcendental-no-change people and clearly show this mind set. Think about the Shakers, or some of the Amish and Mennonites. Such groups are good illustrations of the transcendental-no-change mentality.

But early Lutherans in America were not transcendental no-change. They were cut from a different cloth! These people did amazing things, improvising all kinds of variations on their European heritage in the new land. Lutheranism has never been livelier or more imaginative than it was during the first few decades of its many arrivals in America. Each new group of immigrants brought a fresh gust of the improvisational spirit! These people had the audacity to start seminaries in log cabins; they invented new styles of congregational polity; they learned how to initiate new congregations without the support of a state tax; early pastors took great, sweeping missionary tours through wild country opening new congregations all along the way without ever knowing how their work would continue. These are only some of the things transcendental change people did. Their mark is all over the church even of today. The TNC people were not useless in this period. As quickly as TC people developed something new, TNC people cast the new in concrete and in that way prepared a tradition for a church which had no real history. That's important, too. But the TNC role lacks the flair of that of TC.

The other two initials, *SC* and *SNC* stand for *secular change* and *secular no-change*. The term *secular change* refers to people who develop their understanding of a situation, or who establish their attitudes toward life, by using all kinds of non-theological philosophies. Some might guide their life and decisions by Jeffersonian principles of democracy, by humanism, by the writings of men like Eric Hoffer, or whatever "liberating" philosophy has the intellectual upper hand. People motivated by secular concepts can be very moral and remarkably enthusiastic for good. Their goals may appear to be identical to those of transcendental-change people, but the motivation is different. That difference in motivation can cause considerable misunderstanding—even confusion. For instance, the secular-change person and the transcendental-change person may both vote affirmatively to expand the congregation's efforts among some minority group in the community, but the reason for the action is crucial to the decision. If the secular-change person does so because he believes in minority rights as a democratic principle, his decision is very different from that of the transcendental-change person who may believe in minority rights because of a brotherhood that grows from God's great redemptive act in Christ Jesus. While normally there isn't much tension between secular-change people and transcendental-change people, the issues that are being considered in any given moment have a great effect on the way a secular-change person may vote, or the things he may say. Secular-change people don't talk a lot about world missions, nor do they always understand what it means to edify and upbuild a person in Christ Jesus.

And the secular-no-change person? He is the Archie Bunker type. As he puts it, "I don't want nothing to change." He wants a church he has casually supported, and only seldom used, to stay the way he thinks it has always been, even if he believes it doesn't serve any useful purpose! That's Archie! And after 20 years of pastoral ministry, I've come to the conclusion that many Archies are members of our finest Lutheran churches! He seldom comes to meetings, but when he does, you really know he is present. To my further dismay, I've even seen him occasionally looking back at me from my shaving mirror!

Now, in case any of us think that everyone can be easily slotted into one of these four positions, let me hasten to say that all four forces are struggling for prominence, in all of us, all of the time. There are things about which I am TNC (why did they have to change the tune to my favorite hymn—a hymn I have known and loved so much for such a long period of time?). There's a certain amount of SC in me that generally crops up when a practical matter is to be decided in congregational life (we had better pay the custodian the Federal minimum wage because if we don't someone may take us into court and question our tax-exempt status). I hope the predominant force active in my life is that of TC, and that I am empowered by the Holy Spirit to move forward in Christ Jesus, concerned only with the need of the hour and the demanding mission of the church. In my darkest moments I am strictly SNC. Out of petulence, or frustration, or just plain meanness, I work to scuttle things that are going on. In my secular-no-change moods I don't like the color of the bulletin, I'm unimpressed with the junior choir, I am against the constitutional revisions, I balk at the new red robes of the acolytes. All for no reason.

Pause for a few moments and ask yourself, "At which point of the square do I spend most of my time?" And after you have spent time thinking about yourself, turn your attention to your congregation. Ask the question, "At which point of the square does our congregation seem to spend the most of its time?"

Now how do we deal with all this? Can people

change? How? The most exciting thing is that we *can* deal with it. And, yes, people can be changed!

Transcendental people have a commitment to the Word of God. They can be talked to in Christian terms. What they often lack is an understanding of their world.

Take the time with transcendental-no-change people to explain the usefulness of change in this world. Help them understand that the course proposed is not inconsistent with the Word of God or the cause of Christ, and then patiently show them how change can be a blessing.

With the secular person one must press the positive claim of the Christian faith, "Thus says the Lord . . . . " He must understand the sweeping claim of our Lord Jesus Christ, the reality of regeneration, the gift of justification, the divine possibilities of sanctification. That's why even the most practical meetings of the church ought to begin with prayer and ought never wander very far from the Word of God. There is nothing more "practical" than the life in Christ or more down-to-earth than Scripture. That life in Christ takes into consideration everything the world knows, *plus* everything that God has shown us in his revelation. The combination of those two makes us far more capable of fighting the fight of faith effectively.

Lutherans and the World

You won't find those four initials in *A Study of Generations*. But they are closely woven through three dimensions which are crisply identified in the book. These three dimensions are prevalent among Lutherans. These dimensions are (1) a desire for a *dependable world,* (2) a desire for a *controllable world,* and (3) a desire for *detachment from the world.*

A *dependable world* is one which is stable, orderly, and predictable. Most Lutherans are inclined to desire a dependable world, but not strongly so. People who score highly in this dimension are very interested in morality. They like to preserve what is good from the past. They are not opposed to change, but they do want change to occur in an orderly fashion. They have characteristics of both transcendental change *and* transcendental no-change, with a heavier commitment to no-change.

The distinctive quality of those who desire a *controllable world* is that they have a preference for a world they can help shape. These are people who prefer vigorous robust action, who have an open exuberant attitude toward the world. Change is accepted as valuable. The number of members of our church who desire a controllable world is about the same as those who desire a dependable world, with a slightly greater tendency to prefer a controllable world.

The final group of Lutherans are those who have a sense of deep *detachment from the world.* They are a minority — but a very present minority — including about 5% of our total active membership. They value passivity and non-involvement. They aren't aiming for a life of self-indulgence, but rather for increased insight into themselves. Their goal is to abandon the world and absorb the self into communion with all that God is, often to the total exclusion of human needs and God's intent for the here-and-now.

54

How About Your Parish?

A look at the world view of Lutherans-in-general presents that kind of picture. Of greatest importance to you, right now, is how this information affects your congregation. So let's talk about it and see what we can deduce about your parish. Discuss these questions. If you work hard at them, you'll be rewarded!

1. Using the TC/TNC/SC/SNC formula, where do you think you fit most of the time? We asked that question earlier, but now try to discuss it, with others, in the light of the three additional dimensions from *A Study of Generations*.

2. Using the TC/TNC/SC/SNC formula, where does your congregation fit most of the time? What makes you think so?

3. Looking at your congregation from the perspective of those who want to control the world, those who want a dependable world, and those who want to be detached from the world, which force dominates in your parish life?

4. Pick out some congregational effort of the past year that you think succeeded. What role did the various segments of your congregation play in its success?

5. Pick out something in your congregational effort of the past year which you think failed. Recognizing the different forces in the parish, how may that effort have been reshaped to give it a better chance for achievement?

If someone had explained the four parts of the square to me early in my ministry (and had then outlined the three dimensions which were operable in Lutheran congregations), I believe I could have been a much more effective pastor. I also believe that the church councils with which I served would have done a much more effective job of leading. My preaching would certainly have been different. Some of the programs which the church council proposed would have died aborning, and others would have been given the twist necessary to make them succeed. The more we know about our people and the way they think, the better we understand them, the more effective will be our ministry in them and through them.

Keep in mind that there is more than one Lutheran view of life. If you forget, you will forever be upset by decisions of the group which, from time to time, will confuse you — and may even make you angry. Instead, armed with insight, you'll be a better leader.

5

You Are
What You Believe

On the wall of a classroom I visited was a colorful health poster. In large letters, reinforced with appropriate illustrations, it carried the message: *You are what you eat!* That's a clue to understanding the distinctiveness of Lutherans. Change only one word in that health slogan and you have it: *You are what you believe!* That's what the authors of *A Study of Generations* concluded. Men act, as they act, on the basis of what they believe. The distinctive quality of Lutheranism doesn't lie in its worship forms, or its hymn melodies, or its church architecture, or its congregational polity. The distinctive quality of Lutherans is directly related to what we believe. Believing includes how we hang our teachings together, and how we share those convictions in our practice. The ultimate test of what a person believes is what he does. Nothing speaks as eloquently as the deed!

What Do Lutherans Believe?

The authors of *A Study of Generations* write, "The doctrines Lutherans hold most firmly are belief in the virgin birth of Jesus, the historical resurrection of Jesus, the vicarious atonement of Jesus, the real presence of Jesus in the Eucharist, and the Ten Commandments as God's law." Those doctrines may or may not be what thousands of Lutheran pastors have been trying to communicate to their congregations through the years, but those are the doctrines which are most commonly held by Lutherans *of all synodical groups.*

In evaluating the theological attitude of Lutherans, the authors state, "The weight of Lutheranism is on a conservative belief system, neither fundamentalistic nor liberal." They write further, "Lutherans show a very strong awareness of God's providential care," and "As a group Lutherans express certainty of faith and good feelings about the practice of worship, prayer, and sharing the faith." Finally, "He knows there is more to life than what he can feel, see, smell, hear, or taste."

A paragraph in Chapter 5 of *A Study of Generations* wraps it up. "As a group, most Lutherans say they believe in the historical truth of the birth of Jesus of a virgin, his death, and his actual resurrection at the tomb. They believe in the Bible as God's Word and the law of God as a guide and judge of men's lives. They believe in Christ's death as an atonement for sin. They believe in the gifts of the Spirit, Baptism, the reality of the Eucharist, the return of Christ, and God's response to intercessory prayer. They do not accept a simple categorical view of human nature, that man is totally depraved, but rather prefer a more complex understanding. They do not hold a simple view of the

58

Office of Ministry and the power to forgive sins, but rather prefer a more complex idea. They do not hold the view that the theory of evolution is contrary to the Christian faith. In short, Lutherans maintain the historic quality of the faith, basing it upon the reality of Christ's birth, death, and resurrection, and believing it to be the way of salvation. They are unwilling to say that there is only one true visible church to which every Christian must belong."

Chapter 5 of *A Study of Generations,* "The Heart of Lutheran Piety," is crucial to any pastor's understanding of how his ministry should be shaped and any church council's view of its role as theological leaders. To initiate activities, or maintain a ministry which conflicts with the credal statements of Luther and the conviction of most members of our church, would, at the very least, call into question the right of any parish to claim the name Lutheran. More significantly it comprises our claim to be Christian. And if there is one thing Lutherans claim, it is their right to be called Christian!

In summarizing the chapter the authors write, "We know that most Lutherans hold to transcendental meaning in life. The heart of Lutheran piety includes knowledge of a personal, caring God who loves men in Jesus Christ. There is a sense of certainty in faith. The content of belief runs toward a conservative, traditional, doctrinal stance with most emphasis upon the personal work of Jesus.

"There is an accepting, hopeful attitude toward death. There is an emotional dimension that accepts religious experience but does not emphasize it highly. The exclusive truth claim of Christianity is accepted

59

and upheld, while an exaggerated identification of truth with the church is rejected. While faith has consequences in personal feeling in life, a Christian Utopia is not terribly attractive. Salvation by works is rejected. Values focus on self-development are rejected. The gospel is known. Christ is the center of faith. There is still a Christian mind among us."

Now, while it's all still fresh in your mind, take Luther's explanation of the Apostles' Creed, and measure his words against the description of the Lutheran mind as *A Study of Generations* describes it. Is anything missing? Check it out, concept-by-concept.

Now to Your Meeting

It's time to talk about the implications of this important chapter. Let me try a few questions. The first is both the simplest and the most difficult. Simply put, the question reads, "Is yours really a Lutheran congregation?" What do you have to say about it? What if it isn't? How can we tell? Dare we wonder?

To determine whether any of us are Lutheran, we can look to our congregational statements of faith and to our own reasons for taking on the name Lutheran. First dig out a copy of your constitution and complete statements 1 and 2. Then search your heart and complete statement 3.

1. Our constitution states that our congregational faith is based on, and expressed by . .
2. The purpose of this congregation is constitutionally expressed in the words . .
3. I belong to this church as a way of saying I believe in . . .

Those are three places to review the stated reason

for your congregational existence *and* your personal conviction. Both reviews are important. Is there anything distinctively Lutheran about those three statements as you have completed them? Would non-Lutherans be likely to say the same things? Could non-Christians share your convictions? How you respond will help you to isolate the distinctively Lutheran character of your congregation—and of you.

To further highlight our concern for what it means to be Lutheran, let's get down to specifics. Following are a series of practical applications of your Lutheran faith commitment. How do you deal with them? Let the individual in your church council primarily responsible for the congregational activity in the area answer first, and then the rest of you chime in.

Stewardship: "Our congregational stewardship program is Lutheran. I can state this because . . . ." What *would* you state? Is the love of Christ (my love for Christ, and his love for me) the motivation for stewardship which your parish uses? Is lifting the level of each member's commitment to Christ more important, in practice, than raising the budget? What kind of stewardship approaches do you think really get "results"? Why do you feel so? Are these approaches Lutheran, or do you use them because they seem to work?

Education: "If there is one thing unique about the Lutheran view on education it is . . . ." What is the Lutheran view of education? How is your conviction of this reflected in the way you choose and train teachers? How is it reflected in the methods you use to motivate students, in the way you select your class materials, or in the kind of facilities you provide for teaching and learning?

61

Property: "When people pass our church they know we are Lutheran by the . . . . " Is the maintenance of your church facility reflective of your theology? Is the very existence of your buildings a reflection? What does the appearance of your church plant tell others about what you believe?

Finance: "The financial philosophy of this congregation is one which shows what it means to be Lutheran because . . . . " What's the relationship between when, how, and why you pay your bills, and the life in Christ? Does your budget show Lutheran priorities? How does the way you invest your monies and use them reflect your commitment to a Lutheran theology? Is there a distinctive Lutheran attitude in this area?

Evangelism: "We have a Lutheran evangelism program. You can tell that by the attitude we have toward . . . . " Why do we have an evangelism program in our congregation? Who is involved with it? Whom are we seeking? Whom do we send? What do they say? What do we expect to happen because of your evangelism effort?

As you discuss these things be wary of minimizing motivation, of glossing over the obvious (at least obvious to you), and also of discounting your effectiveness. *A Study of Generations* makes it clear that the majority of Lutherans have a distinctive and deeply Christian quality to their faith and life. We want to identify those qualities not only in general, but also in specific. We want to rejoice in them, build on them, and share them with the world that men might "believe that Jesus is the Christ, the Son of God, and that believing they might have life through his name" (John 20:31).

6

Twentieth-Century Dynamite: Social Issues

An outstanding documentary of the 1960s is *A Time for Burning*. The film follows the struggle of a congregation in Omaha as it came to grips with questions of racism and its effects on the parish. Many church members squirmed as this real-life story of bigotry, angry congregational struggle, moral uncertainty, and excruciating soul-searching unfolded on the screen. Some asked, "Could this really be happening in my church?" Our average church member came to understand that it could. And not only was it happening in the Omaha church, but he suspected the same potential for tension nestled uneasily in his own congregation, as well.

The late 1960s, and early 1970s, forced all of us to confront an aspect of life we were most reluctant to face. That aspect is a category of concern called "social issues." In those years, Christians saw church councils, congregational meetings, even area and national church conventions struggle with the proper role of the church in face of social issues. For some the proper role was no-role-at-all. For others the only proper role was total involvement. All the way—whatever that meant! They wanted that involvement backed by the church's total resources of manpower and money, plus a public witness on behalf of social consciousness. Housing, government, war, hunger, distribution of wealth, public health policies, welfare, the many faces of discrimination, and a dozen other topics fell within the broad framework of social issues.

The struggle reached such intensity that some members of congregations left their church in anger and disgust. Others revised (both upwards and downwards) their financial support for the denomination. Some even worked to force their pastor out of the parish ministry. Another group organized to capture positions of institutional power within the church. Some acted as they did in order to stop the trend toward what they called "a godless social gospel." Others organized with equal vigor on behalf of what they called a fully responsible Christian ministry. The fight went on and on. This struggle is not over yet. For some it is just beginning.

The Church's Record

An interesting footnote to all this is the surprise shown by some that their church would even consider participation in a discussion of social issues. The further suggestion that the church ought to become financially and institutionally involved was overwhelming. How quickly we forget! The history of the development of the church, and the history of the development of social consciousness, are intertwined. For example, in the centuries gone by the church played a leading part in developing such things as the rules of chivalry. Wandering knights were urged *by the church* to lift themselves above the more normal practice of crushing the weak, ravaging the lands, and dominating the powerless, and, instead, accept a responsibility toward those who are unable to care for themselves. From that view, pressed by the church, Sir Galahad and his friends developed their considerably more humane rules of knightly conduct. In another area of human interchange the church of the past said there was a better way to deal with those who had committed crimes than to execute them, or to throw them into dungeons, or maim them by torture and physical abuse. Out of those people of God came the idea of the reformatory and the penitentiary. "Reforming" people and giving them an opportunity for "true penitence" beat the heartless brutality of their age—and sounded as strange in that time as the most advanced suggestion of social change today.

Who do you think conceived of orphanages as a way for helping homeless children to grow up with at least some of the advantages of those whose parents were yet living? And what, would you suppose, was the moving force behind the establishment of homes for the aged, leprosariums, hospitals, and other institutional responses to human ills? The church, of course! The church of the Middle Ages accepted the task of education at the elementary level—and the levels of higher education, as well. We'd be hard-pressed to mention a college established in North America before the 1800s which did not have its beginning by the church. Add to these things the continued interest of the church with the plight of the socially disadvantaged, the institutionalized, the hungry and the naked, and you have an amazing picture of Christianity's long and continued concern for things which are called "social issues."

Get yourself in the right frame of mind for some discussion of the church and social issues by taking a few moments right now to list any agency, or institution, or program of a national church which had its beginning, before 1940, in response to a social need. Begin with your immediate community. Then expand your scope to include the regional area in which your congregation exists. Finally, list any national Lutheran organizations that were responsive to a distinctive social need of that bygone age.

That should be quite a list. But that's what others did. What are *we* ready to do?

And Today?

For an answer *A Study of Generations* probed the mood and temperament of the Lutheran church of our time with regard to social issues. They developed a number of insights into contemporary Lutheran attitudes toward social issues based on the questions they asked and the answers they received. Here are a few.

1. 70% of all Lutherans think the church has a twofold task: first, to preach the gospel; but second, to improve the well-being of people. The overwhelming

majority believe that preaching the gospel is the *primary* task, but not the exclusive task. In this regard many Lutherans, especially youth, say that too little attention is given to a concern for the well-being of people.

2. Most Lutherans reflect a liberal stance on social issues and express a commitment to the goal of a just and responsible society. The picture of Lutherans as opposed to matters of social improvement, or insensitive to social concerns, lacks support in the findings of *A Study of Generations.* To help you grasp this view of Lutherans, think for a moment of how many of our "liberal" governors, senators, representatives, and mayors who are Lutheran, or who come from areas with a significant, even predominant, Lutheran population. There are quite a few! But that should surprise no one. Our forefathers were deeply involved with social issues from the time they set foot on these shores. In those days *they* were the abused segment of our population. For that reason, and based on their beliefs, many of our earliest church papers contain vigorous and involved discussions of a rich variety of social issues. You'd be surprised at some of the positions they proposed and supported!

3. The tension in the Lutheran church is not between those who have and don't have deep social concerns, but whether, and in what way, the institutional church should be involved in those social concerns. It is about the level of involvement of the church body—the national denomination, the regional segments, or the local congregation—that the sharp divisions of opinion develop.

4. Lutherans permit their pastors personal involvement in matters of social concern. They even look to them for leadership. But they do not want this leadership exerted from the pulpit. The pulpit, in the minds of most Lutherans, is not the place for the enunciation of personal positions regarding specific social concerns. Within small groups? Yes! By face-to-face discussion? Yes! In committees and organized concern groups of the congregation? Yes! Within the context of preaching? No!

5. Sixty percent of the Lutherans feel they have a sense of conscience, a sense of personal responsibility, and a sense of personal obligation in matters of social concern. They look to their church to help them become more compassionate, caring Christians. More than 60% of Lutherans are willing to participate in programs of community and church activity. Of this total percentage 24% are now involved, and 36% more would be willing to serve, *if they were asked*.

6. The most vehement resistance to caring about people and to working toward effecting immediate social change comes from those members who are essentially law-oriented. Law-oriented people need unchanging structures and they tend to distrust others. (For further discussion of this read *Bias and the Pious* by James E. Dittes.)

7. Pastors, in general, score higher on the scale of social concern than do the laity, in general. Younger pastors score the highest of all.

8. Those likely to score the lowest on the scale of social concern are laymen who report that they have

never gone to Sunday school during the period of their church membership.

9. Recognizing the sizeable majority of those who are committed to a social concern, we can look forward to increased involvement in social issues by our people. This increased involvement will certainly affect tomorrow's style of mission and ministry.

What Does This Mean?

When we put together all the pieces which *A Study of Generations* places before us, the picture is quite clear. The majority of Lutherans care about others in our society, and they want to do something positive to help those in need. They see the church as a place where they can be trained and equipped for compassionate caring, and they see it as a divine vehicle for helping them develop and maintain a sympathetic emotional stance to the needs of others. They may, or may not, want the church, itself, to be actively involved in matters of social concerns. If they are convinced that the proclamation of the gospel is not compromised, they can be undisturbed by the involvement of the church in matters of social concern. The typical Lutheran believes his Christian life style ought to have, and will have, an effect upon society, but he is most comfortable in one-to-one involvement rather than as part of a mass movement. But, don't forget that within the Lutheran family there is a minority who feel very different and sharply disagree with all of this.

The ones who are opposed to almost any social involvement are a distinct minority, but a *substantial* minority. They reject any kind of institutional concern for social ills, or any confrontation of social issues, except as they might develop within a very limited range of needs. This minority individual is basically quite pessimistic about his own life and his own life style. He is distinctly inclined toward being prejudiced. He does not believe that the church will be able to change anything in our society, nor does he expect it to try. According to *A Study of Generations,* this individual is probably middle-aged, limited in the amount of education he has received, and on the basis of congregational seniority may very possibly be a member of your church council.

What Does This Mean for Your Congregation?

I visited a congregation only a few years ago which carried on a two-level conversation with me during my visit. On the one hand the parish was deeply disturbed by what they thought was going on in the national church. In a variety of different ways they let me know that in their opinion the church was "too involved in social issues." They offered occasional specifics to undergird their opinion. The specifics were generally cast in rather biting comments about race, laziness on the part of the poor, and a conviction that welfare is abused by most.

At the same time I was able to piece together quite another story from the recitation of life in their parish. In a very wonderful way, for many years, this congregation had been deeply involved in the needs of its own community. Involvement included participation in actually building part of the high school, a proven sensitive concern for the aged, much direct help to those in physical need, the initiation of community programs for remedial reading, and a unique kind of job-training which developed at their instigation. When I pointed out the apparent contradiction between their horridly judgmental words, and their commendable social-action deeds, they showed great surprise. One man said, "What we've been doing isn't social action! We've just been neighborly!" Could it be that many of us haven't seen the relationship between what it means to be neighborly and what it means to work for social justice? Could be. Let's struggle together with some questions in that general area, to see what might develop.

Back at the Meeting

1. What role do your congregational educational activities play in developing social consciousness among your people? Congregational educational activities include Sunday school, Bible classes, various discussion groups, parochial schools, and the rich variety of other methods of educational communication which congregations use.

Evidently some very fine things are happening in our Sunday schools! To see what's happening, review the songs your children sing in Sunday school. What themes do they contain? Then take a look at the Sunday school lessons. Do these songs and lessons sensitize our people to social concern?

Just for fun, study the story of The Good Samaritan and try to make a modern application that *does not* get involved with some aspect of social concern. Make a list of commonly taught Bible stories which, while they may not primarily teach us something about living with each other in a more responsible way, at least indirectly suggest that we care for one another. Remembering that Lutherans don't like specific applications to social concerns from the pulpit, what other means are used in our congregations to expand or otherwise sensitize our people to what it means to be alive in our world today?

2. Lutherans are very responsive to specific and proven examples of social need. They agree that there is no point in bewailing the abuses of welfare in New York City when their primary perimeter of concern is Eureka, Kansas. To help focus your discussion draw a circle, perhaps ten miles in diameter, using your congregation as the center. Look at that area. What are the pressing social concerns (call them "needs for neighborliness") that are obvious? How are the aged, poor, jobless, infirm, hospitalized, young, doing? How does the migrant worker, ex-prisoner, reformed alcoholic, drug addict, inadequately housed family fare? Talk about it a while and then tighten your circle of concern. What are the problems within a mile of your church, even six blocks? Rather than generalize, take the time to list some of the specific concerns you feel are genuine and need attention.

3. What are you going to do about this? Look within your church. Is there any person, or persons, who can help your sensitizing process or become the key person in effecting a necessary and useful social change? Your people *do* desire to help in matters of this type. But how can they be involved? The most promising category for consideration are those 36% who stated

that their assistance is available *if asked*. What does that say about our more usual Lutheran approach to enlisting assistance by calling for volunteers? Do we need a new method of enlistment, or a better one? Could our method for enlisting help be the reason why only a few appear to be deeply involved in most activities for the church? In your congregation, there is a large group who are ready to pitch in, but who need someone to ask them for their help. Maybe it's time for us to quit complaining about the number unwilling to give assistance, and acknowledge that some people need a bit more direction. Or, that some people have a personality which holds them back from volunteering. Or, that we have done a less-than-adequate job of enlisting and educating people for greater service. To help you in this broad area of discussion, talk about these questions: How did you get involved? Were you asked? By whom?

4. How good a reading of your congregation have you made? Do you really know their attitudes in a variety of areas of social concern? *A Study of Generations* tells us that Lutherans heavily support the contention that racial discrimination should end and that the church should help toward achieving that goal. How would that fit your parish? In another area of social concern, slightly more than 50% of our people believe that *all* war is morally wrong. In yet another area, 9 out of 10 feel that social deviations, like alcoholism and drug addiction, are diseases that should be treated as such. Does that sound like Lutherans no longer view drunkenness as a sin, or could it be that they view drunkenness as a sin which we must help control?

All in all, most Lutherans have a rather open stance toward social issues. The conclusions of the authors of *A Study of Generations* is that, "Lutherans on the whole have a commitment to a just and liberalized society. If they're going to fight, it will be about whether the church institution itself should be an active participant, or whether it should leave its members free to participate as individual citizens." How would that analysis fits your parish?

5. In what way is your parish presently involved with matters of social concern? Make a list of all the agencies or activities your congregation supports. Include in this list institutions like colleges, homes for retarded, schools for the deaf, rest homes, or homes for the aged. Do you have a Meals-on-Wheels activity in your area (that's a program for preparing hot meals for the home-bound aged)? Do you support FISH or HELP (activities to help local emergency needs in housing, food and clothing), DIAL-A-TEEN (telephone answering service for teenagers who need someone to talk with)? Is your pastor involved in counseling beyond the congregational membership level? Does he participate in chaplaincy work at jails, hospitals, or other institutions? Add to your list the various emergency needs to which you as a congregation has responded in the last two years. List things like blood drives, Lutheran World Relief clothing drives, help for people who have suffered from floods, hurricanes, earthquakes, and other disasters. Finally, how about the individual assistance your parish has given to specific people of your community offering them money, food, advice, or assistance of any kind. It may even help you grasp the scope of your congregation's activ-

ity by asking members to fill out a questionnaire on their personal and private levels of involvement. Do they support CARE, Red Cross, United Fund, HOPE, and the hundreds of other worthwhile endeavors which surround us? Add them up. It will help you understand your own congregation. It will help your congregation answer charges about the level of concern which Christians have for the world's needs.

The question of Lutheran involvement in social issues or in social concerns is not one of whether, but one of how, and how much. By the same token, the primary question facing a church council, or a parish pastor, is one of how they will help such action take place, and whether they will consciously exert a direct and supportive hand in the action.

For some any discussion of the church's involvement in social issues is explosive and potentially divisive. For level-headed Lutherans it's generally a matter of talking about normal neighborliness. What's it like in your church?

7

Differences:
How to Live with Them

In the late '60s I spent considerable time traveling around the United States speaking to various groups about our church. To set the stage for group discussion, I picked up a little device for triggering response. Did it ever work! I would distribute to the gathered group two incomplete sentences and ask them to finish these sentences by adding the first comparison that came to their mind. How about doing the same thing, right now? Try it, please.

1. The church as I have come to know it is like a . . .

2. The church as God intended it should be like a . . .

Those are the sentences. Did you put down your first thought?

I was fascinated, everywhere, by the answers that

rolled in. They were remarkably similar, often identical. The most common completion of the first sentence was, ". . . a sleeping giant," ". . . a wilted flower," ". . . a polluted river." The "sleeping giant" answer was far and away the most common. It kept coming through no matter what the group, or where the group was meeting in the United States. Then came variations on the other two, followed by all kinds of other essentially negative evaluations. Rarely did a participant compare the church to anything positive.

The second sentence was a different story. It was always completed with a quite positive comparison: ". . . the bride of Christ," ". . . a shining light," ". . . a family," were some of the more common responses.

If the people attending these meetings had been congregational delinquents, back-sliders, passive parish participants, or the like, I might have understood their responses. But the people who came to the meetings at which I spoke were more often leaders in their congregation, committed Lutheran Christians, people who were interested enough to make the special effort to attend. If anything, a person would reasonably expect a response of dewy-eyed optimism or exaggerated confidence from them. But that's not what came through. Why the dour, even negative, attitude?

How Lutherans See the Church

A Study of Generations gets at this general concern by offering insights into our typical Lutheran's view of his church. Here are some conclusions.

1. To begin, the individual Lutheran makes very lit-

tle psychological distinction between family life and congregational life. The individual's church and the individual's family are viewed alike. Both are seen as having similar characteristics in mattters such as "caring for others," or "a commitment to broad social issues." While most of our members feel quite positively toward these and similar items, 20% have a very dismal view of their congregational *and* family life. Of these 5% quite emphatically reject any positive understanding of church *and* family life. Are they reacting to what they see in the church, or what they see in their family? Since I first read about this I've wondered what would have happened if I had asked the groups, referred to earlier, for completion of the sentence, "My family as I have come to know it is like . . . . " I suspect the same three responses would have surfaced! Do you agree?

2. Both our younger Lutherans (teens) and our older Lutherans (post-55) feel the church isn't meeting their needs. When much of the church program is built upon the unconscious assumption that the basic unit of the church is the family, those who do not have a family unit of their own (younger Lutherans and older Lutherans feel their needs are not being recognized. Now check again. What percentage of your parish fits in either the "younger" or "older" category? How do you respond to them?

3. One-fifth of all Lutherans state that they believe the church has nothing to do with real life. Because they feel this way they are ready to abandon support of church-related colleges and church-related agencies believing these extensions of the church are either useless or ineffective. Even more unsettling, they think

the church is blind or ineffective, that it is money-grubbing, cold, and heartless. Beside the 20% who clearly state this, another 5-11% would be inclined to agree with these statements. If they are right, we had better change. If they are wrong, how did they get these opinions, and what can be done to enlighten their view?

4. One-half of all Lutherans feel there is too great a stress in the church on money. One-third believe that no one would know, or would care, if they dropped out. Think of that! The first group of 50% is serious enough, but that group of 33% is really sad. Could they be your younger and older members? Can we afford to rest while one-third of our members feel as they do?

5. *A Study of Generations* shows that specific complaints are not isolatable. Complaints can't be approached and resolved one-by-one. Negative feelings are interlocked. When the member's stance is negative, it does not show itself as just one complaint. Negativism has many faces. When any one complaint is resolved, another grievance will replace it. The authors' conclusion? "The problem is not issues, questions, or programs. It is people." Isn't that fortunate! We're not all that good at resolving issues, or answering questions, or developing programs. But the church, in and through its mission and message, knows how to minister to people. Have we forgotten to do what we do best? I don't think so. But, maybe, we've forgotten how crucial one-to-one ministry really is.

6. All things considered, Lutherans over 24 years of age rate the program of ministry by the church quite

high. Of those under 24 years of age, two-thirds give a basically positive evaluation to their church, and the congregation to which they belong. We have a positive disposition with which to work and on which to build.

7. Negative evaluations of the church, and a companion discontent with the congregation, are closely linked to the individual member's doubt in the area of *certainty of faith*. It is important to note that generally speaking those who are markedly unhappy with their church are also markedly unsettled in their personal faith. That means that each member's personal *theology* is crucial to our life together. We don't necessarily need more and better programs; we need more and better teaching, preaching, and sharing of our faith in Christ and his redemptive work.

8. *A Study of Generations* reveals that a Lutheran congregation consists of many subgroups. They contrast enough in their values and priorities to make tension a normal experience and the acceptance of diversity a constant requirement. The single greatest source of tension in the church is a difference in values and beliefs of the church members. (Reread that sentence. It shatters any view of the congregation built on the assumption of theological unanimity!) A second source of tension relates to age differences (not only is there validity to the teenager's complaint that his parents don't understand him, but it's equally true that he doesn't understand his parents). The third most significant source of tension is the difference in the amount of education. (Education can hinder or help communication and understanding—both ways!)

81

9. The age of 21-22 is the low-watermark in belief. There is a steady decline in belief from 15 to 21 years of age, but from 21 to 30 there is a very sharp rise followed by a steady increase to age 65. Less than half our youth live with a sense of gospel awareness, and they lack positive conviction in areas of a certainty of faith, awareness of a personal and caring God, and a positive attitude toward life and death. Now, I ask you, who should be youth counselors? Should it be "someone their own age?" Or is this the place for your most mature Christian member?

What Does This All Mean?

To gather *all* of the areas of difference, and *all* of the areas of Christian concern, an individual would have to read, and carefully study, the entirety of *A Study of Generations*. I believe that those who can, should. But, even these few items cited suggest some very definite things about a congregation and its members.

For one thing, we should never view our church or congregation as a monolithic structure in which everyone holds the same convictions with the same degree of intensity. The church is a mixture of many attitudes and forces. Different people are at markedly different points on the span of faith. Age, educational level, and the intensity of personal convictions vigorously flavor the congregational average.

While most Lutherans are very happy with their life (they say they would choose nine more lives just like the one which they have known), some are distinctly unhappy. They show this discontent not only in their

feelings of personal unhappiness, but also in their attitude toward the church, its effectiveness, and its direction. It is very important that the church council, and
the pastor, identify the intensity of these negative feelings in any given parish. It is only then that a truly
responsive ministry can be developed—one that mean-
ingfully responds to those specific needs of the individuals and those segments of the congregation which
most need attention. If the council doesn't volun-
tarily take the time to do this, it will be involuntarily
forced to do so. When nearly half the members are
in personal pain or are confused about their goals, few
things work well and some things won't work at all!

Some Pastoral Observations

Pertinent to the insights of *A Study of Generations*,
I recall some very distinctive conclusions which developed in my ministry. I didn't have the kind of supportive documentation which *A Study of Generations*
provides, but certain operative principles began to
surface as my years of ministry increased. One such
set of conclusions had to do with young people.

I learned that when I was counseling with a teenager, the most stimulating beginning to our conversation would be for me to ask, "Do you like yourself?"
At first the answer surprised me. After a while I came
to expect it. With a very few exceptions the response
was, "No." As the conversation developed, they would
almost all point out what should have been obvious
to me. They would mention how much time and effort
adults exert in urging teen-agers to become something
different from what they are. Mothers and fathers call

this *training* or *education*. Young people call it *criticism*. My typical teen-age friend finally continued, "If all that effort is being exerted to make me be something other than what I am, I must not be worth much in my present state."

Another little insight which developed in counseling with youngsters who had gotten into trouble (that included everything from shoplifting to general insubordination in school) was that there was always "someone else" lurking in the background. While there must be an exception somewhere, there was never one in my experience. It seemed that nobody ever got in trouble by themselves. Identifying that "someone else" and helping young persons understand the part the other person played in the development of their problem was a large part of the counseling experience. Those warnings in the Book of Proverbs about carefully choosing companions are appropriate.

These two little insights are examples of what surfaces when you are modestly observant, a bit curious, slightly sensitive, and unencumbered with the burden that you already know everything. I'm sure you have many insights every bit as valid—and much more significant. What have you "discovered" about congregational life, or ministry?

Let's see what happens, now, when we endeavor to apply some of the conclusions of *A Study of Generations* to various experiences of congregational life. Be ready to include your own insights. First of all, let's talk about *education*.

Is there a place in the educational process of your congregation for the youngster whose chronological and spiritual age do not coincide? This usually shows

84

itself when a youngster says, "Sunday school is boring." Are there a variety of educational approaches practiced in your parish—a variety which recognizes the youngsters' variety of interests? Or does everyone in the same age group get the same kind of teaching experience regardless of interest and human uniqueness? And what about the older members? Are there a rich variety of educational experiences possible? How many different kinds of educational groupings do you try to offer? To put this whole section into a perspective, in what are the congregational educational offerings responsive to that diversity which is a real part of your congregational family? To help your discussion with each other, list the different kinds of educational groupings your congregation offers (Sunday school, Bethel Bible Series, etc.).

Now list the different methods of education which your congregation utilizes (lecture, group projects, discussion, etc.)

Are you satisfied that your answers represent the best use of present congregational educational opportunities, congregational skills, and congregational facilities? Don't worry about what you could do if you had a larger building—or more teachers—or better material. Talk about that later. Instead focus on present staff, present materials, present skills, present participants, present needs and present opportunities. How are you doing?

From education, let's turn to *worship*. How many different kinds of worship experience does your congregation offer? List them.

Can your congregational worship life bend enough to accommodate the varieties of worship needs which surely must be represented within your congregation? What happens to people who worship in your church but who find chanting disturbing, or those who would love to hear, and derive great benefit from, this traditional style of worship? Do those who find delight in contemporary worship forms have a chance? Is the congregation permitted, even encouraged, to participate in the preparation of meaningful worship experiences? In what way does your worship reflect the varieties of attitude which your congregational members possess? Talk about these things. You can be sure your members do!

From worship we turn to *stewardship*. Why do one-half of our members think that there is too great an emphasis on money in our churches? Does your congregation feel that way? What's fascinating is that about half of our members *don't* share that complaint. It would be easy to say that those who give are committed, and those who don't aren't. Is that what's going through the mind of your parish? To trigger this discussion answer (privately if you wish) these two questions:

1. Have you, personally, increased your offering in the past five years?

2. What reason do you give yourself for either giving more, giving less, or giving about the same?

A study of one of the Lutheran churches developed the following predictors of how much money an individual will give to his church: total family earnings; feelings toward charitable giving; how positive an individual views life; degree to which a voice in spending is desired; feeling toward special appeals; degree of involvement in the church and its activities; age (giving increases with age); education (more education—more tendency to give); commitment to God and belief in him; degree to which giving of money is considered an expression of faith; how regularly an individual gives.

By the same token, the following variables were found to be *unrelated* to giving money to the church: number of dependents in the family; length of membership in the local church; the congregational priorities given to church expenses; specifying funds for particular church programs; consideration of why people give; functions performed by the church; consideration of others losing interest in the church; feelings about importance of the denomination; giving on condition of agreement with the church role; degree of commitment to social concerns.

A careful study of those last two paragraphs would suggest that many stewardship programs falter for very predictable reasons. Review your congregational stewardship effort in the light of those findings.

This study further commented that a thorough reading of stewardship material is directly related to the amount of money given; those who pledge give more than those who do not; members who have been contacted through an Every-Member Visitation program within a two-year period tend to give more than those who have not been visited.

Taking those comments into consideration, what do they have to say to the present stewardship response by members of your congregation?

Adding It All Up

The view a person has toward the church is dependent on many things. The view the church has of the individual is equally dependent on many things. Crucial to a congregational understanding of its life together is a recognition that we do not all stand at the same point of faith, have the same experience, live and work in our Christian life from the same perspective, or share goals with equal intensity. The task of the church is to meet people at the point where they are and strive to edify them. Dealing with people of varying perspectiveness means that you begin with them at the point where they are. It is very Lutheran to believe that God, through his holy Spirit, is doing just that. He is constantly moving and changing people. A careful evaluation of the reality of your congregation, coupled with a solid theological conviction that God wants to and is doing his work in and among us, can set the stage for useful interaction and real growth to the glory of our Lord and for the good of his people.

8

Pastors—
in Another World?

At his death the poet, Robert Frost, was described as a man who had "a lover's quarrel with the world." That delightful way of describing the simultaneous (and seemingly contradictory) emotions of affection and rejection, attraction and devotion, joy and sadness, describes so much of his poetry and his attitude toward the world.

Most churchmen have that same feeling toward the pastoral ministry. As one responsible for the conduct, the needs, the attitudes, and the practices of hundreds of pastors, teachers, deaconesses, full-time lay workers, educational specialists and the like, I, too, live in a middle world of sympathy for, and frustration from, that remarkable band of men and women whom we have called to our professional ministry. No one has joined the church in quite the same way they have. Theirs is no Sunday commitment. Having experienced

the regeneration of baptism, the commitment of confirmation, and the joy of a life in Christ, they have
gone one step further by turning their lives over to the
Lord, and his church, for fulltime use as professional
servants in the preaching and teaching ministry. The
decision to do so was not easy, and the price they are
asked to pay by this determination is no modest sum.
Most are satisfied with their decision, but some want
to renegotiate their contract, either because they are
unable, or unwilling, to live up to its conditions.

What Are They Really Like?

A *Study of Generations* focused on this group, with
particular emphasis on those who have accepted the
pastoral ministry. It makes some interesting observations about clergymen. Some of the conclusions could
be anticipated by any reasonable and sensitive church-
man. Others will come as a bit of surprise. Here are a
few of the results.

1. Clergymen, as a group, have a much longer
work week than those who have similar educational
backgrounds, but who are following another vocation.
A *Study of Generations* shows that 70% of all clergymen work more than 50 hours per week. (Of these
35% work more than 60 hours a week, and 18% more
than 70 hours a week.) By comparison, only 22% of
Lutheran college graduates work more than 50 hours
a week. To come at this insight another way, 39% of
all college graduates in our church work *less* than 40
hours per week, but only 10% of their pastors can ful-
fill their duties in less than 40 hours. It is a simple fact

that ministers work enormously long hours. (And some people think they only work on Sunday!) Consider for a moment what that work load would do to any person in terms of fatigue, of unfulfilled family responsibilities, or pressured judgment in the face of critical decisions, or of overall human effectiveness.

2. 76% of all clergymen receive salaries less than $12,000 a year as compared with 31% of all Lutheran college graduates. That figure includes the total household income. Included in an understanding of that income level must be a recognition of the amount of money each clergyman expended to qualify for the ministry. Until he graduates (often in mid or late 20's), he has had no appreciable income. And if he marries before he graduates, he and his wife must learn to scrimp—an art most will practice during their entire married life.

3. Clergymen, as a group, have a higher commitment to the basic articles of the Christian faith and reflect a more positive view of that faith than does the average layman. Differences between clergymen and the laity are most pronounced when the differences between the male, college graduate, Lutheran layman, and the pastor are isolated. Differences are substantially less when the comparison is made between the female, college graduate, Lutheran member, and the pastor. In addition, there is a much wider latitude of religious commitment among the laity than among the clergy. Interestingly enough, in three dimensions of distinctive content of the Christian faith (Fundamentalism-Liberalism, Christian Utopianism, and The Exclusive Truth Claim of Christianity Exaggerated), there

is no significant difference between the laity and the clergy.

4. There are two doctrines about which there is some difference between the clergy and the laity. One is the doctrine of the nature of man (pastors tend to view the man as inherently evil more than do laymen), and the other is the doctrine of Office of the Keys (pastors affirm that they have the right to forgive repentant sinners, while one in five college graduates reject this aspect of the Office of the Keys).

5. There is some tension between laity and clergymen in the area of the office and the authority of the pastor. Laymen tend to reject the idea that pastors have any kind of unique spiritual power. They tend to see pastors as individuals who help good men in the struggle to live. Pastors have a much broader view of their role.

6. There is a significant difference between laity and clergymen in their understanding of the two natures of Christ. Clergymen accept the unity of the two natures. Laymen readily accept the divinity of Christ, but have trouble in endorsing his humanity. This results in a considerable difference between the laity and clergy with regard to how they view their responsibilities toward the physical needs of men. Clergymen see the church as needing to speak to the whole man, while many laymen see the church's responsibility restricted to a ministry primarily focused on the spiritual dimension of man.

7. One of the sharpest areas of difference between the laity and the clergy is in the area of work righteous-

ness. Clergymen resoundingly reject work righteousness as un-Christian and non-Lutheran. Laymen have a tendency to accept work righteousness as a normal and proper part of their religious existence.

8. Pastors, as a group, are more mobile than are the laity. This is more of a personal observation than a conclusion of *A Study of Generations*. Their finding is that about 8% of Lutherans change their neighborhood each year. When I compare that figure with the pastoral mobility in the district which I serve, and with some conversation on the subject with other synod and district presidents, I cannot help but conclude that pastors are much more mobile than are their members.

9. Most young people would re-style the traditional role of the clergyman, if they could. They would accent a more aggressive approach to the controversial concerns of our day. Yet, even they draw a line at any activity on the part of the clergymen which may result in his arrest. But, parents feel differently about the role of the pastor than do their children. And the pastor stands in between, trying to minister effectively to both.

10. The greatest differences between the clergy and laity occur in the areas of the practice of personal piety, and one's involvement in church and community affairs. The term "practice of personal piety" includes sharing one's faith with another, involvement in church and community affairs, and making one's views known to community leaders. Clergymen recognize this as a significant part of their responsibility, while the laity,

in general, tend to be more passive and self-contained. "Involvement in church and community affairs" means what it says. Pastors are much more committed to responsible action in this area than are laymen.

11. For all that may indicate a difference between the laity and clergy, the overwhelming conclusion of *A Study of Generations* is that they hold many more attitudes and positions in common than attitudes and positions in opposition.

From My Perspective

Based on visits to literally hundreds of churches and as one who has carried on Robert Frost's "lover's quarrel" (only I have directed it toward the clergy more than the world), I share the following observations for comment and discussion:

1. **Pastors must be treasured as an exquisitely precious resource for the church.**

No question about it! Those who have been called to the pastoral office, and who have accepted this call with confidence and joy, must be seen as God's unique and necessary gift to us. I say the same, with equal enthusiasm, of all the thousands who have equipped themselves for service in the church in a multiplicity of ministerial duties ranging from education directors, to teachers, to deaconesses, and to lay workers.

These people are not lazy leeches sucking away at the life blood of the pious and hardworking laity. Springing from the laity (and most servants of the church come from the laity) they have been led by the Spirit to serve God and his people in an unusual way. More than any others who may feel compelled to point it out, they know and recognize the reality of sin in their lives. They know the secret corners of their being—corners which are hidden from all, save the Lord.

Fully conscious of the enormity of their task and the inadequacy of both their training and their personal abilities, these children of God agree to do what some others think is impossible: they agree to bring comfort to the comfortless; hope to the hopeless; peace to the disturbed; confidence to the weak; joy to the depressed; a will to live to those who have long ago given up. They embark on this effort full well knowing that every need to which they are asked to respond is a need which they themselves have; every weakness to which they bring God's judgment is a weakness in which they share; every rebuke they give is just as applicable against themselves; every fear they expose is a fear which they know personally. They bring good news which, because it comes from God, they know is Good News! Without these bearers of his message the shadowy darkness of many a life would dissolve into an inky blackness.

I make bold to speak so glowingly of these servants of the Lord because that's the way they are seen through his eyes. God established the ministry, and God both gave, and gives, the ministry of reconciliation a purpose and a power. You dare not hold the *ministry* of the gospel in less than total awe. While your view of *ministers* may be less inspiring, always remember that those frail humans who have let themselves be used in this service to the gospel must still be seen as a God-given resource.

2. **They are so dreadfully human.**

I wish I knew who first wrote the line: "The church is like Noah's Ark: if it weren't for the storm outside, the smell inside would be overpowering." In that interesting way the anonymous writer recognizes both the worth and the weakness of the church.

The pastoral ministry carries with it the same kind of paradoxical quality of good and bad. Sinful human beings become servants of the Word. Their ordination vows erase none of their inclination to rebellion, error, and transgression—an inclination which touches all who are human. These called servants struggle with the same temptations that have faced all of Adam's sons and daughters, since creation. As common clay they falter in the face of temptation at about the average human rate. They are generally about as perceptive of wisdom, truth, and understanding as any of you who read these words. They have marriage problems, fuss about finances, need vacations, yearn for privacy, feel anger and frustration. Sheltered through much of their growing up period by a system of education that protects them from that which others face early in life, they can be dreadfully immature.

Specializing in a ministry of sensitivity to the needs of your sons and daughters, these same people can be pathetically insensitive in dealing with their own. Wallowing through the complex and often gruesome problems of others, they don't feel they have the right to ask someone to walk with them through their own. They're so human. So very human. But they have as much right to be human as any other person. If only others would minister as directly and lovingly to them as they minister directly and lovingly to the others!

Thank the Lord that almost every parish has one or two marvelous members who sense this condition, and seek to serve the servant of the servants of God. Our pastors, teachers, chaplains, deaconesses, and other servants of God are a precious resource. But don't ever forget that they are a precious resource wrapped in fully human flesh.

3. **Pastors don't always understand laymen.**

I can distinctly remember the excitement I experienced when, while training for the ministry, I kept discovering new and significant things. I'd say to myself, "I'm going to remember how I felt when I discovered this and, as a pastor, help the people I serve find this same wonder!" I still remember how I *felt,* but for the life of me I can't remember what it was that I considered so important. It's like trying to remember how excited you were when you first learned to read, or discovered the potential of the opposite sex, or realized you were no longer a child. Those were all great experiences. You went through them. But can you precisely recapture the glory of those moments when you moved from one world of experience into the other?

For most of us, that movement from one phase of life into the next is a great iron door of dimmed recall which slams behind us, shutting out all that was. Leaving the laity and entering the pastoral office is generally accompanied by such forgetfulness.

For instance, when I became a district president I started commuting to my office as half the men in my parish had done each morning of my 17 years of pastoral ministry. The traffic jams, the frustrating waits, the monotonous repetitive trips along the same streets day after day became an existential routine. It soon dawned on me that while as a parish pastor I "knew" that members of the congregation were commuting (and thought I understood this experience), I didn't really "know." Now, when I go to an evening meeting after that commuting rat-race I notice I am tired, a bit irritable, and occasionally my mind wanders miles away from the matter at hand. It takes me a while to get into the mood of the congregational moment and a bit longer to mentally shift gears to the crisis at hand. As a parish pastor I was *always* in the congregational mood. While others fought traffic, I organized agendas. I was ready and raring to go. I didn't "know" that other weren't.

Pastors often think that laymen fully share their Christian attitudes and they, in turn, fully understand their flock. If some parishioner is dragging his feet in the parish, the pastor can come to believe it's because the members are obstreperous, or testy, or just cantankerous. That's not necessarily so. *A Study of Generations* has identified some fundamental differences between the clergy and the laity. Your pastor may not want to accept them. But you can. Help him acknowledge them and work together with him to confront them. You who are in the majority must know that there probably is one within your group who is the only one who doesn't really understand what it means to be a layman. Help him. You can.

4. Servants of the church live at the point of tension.

The hardest rock is worn down by the steady dripping of water. You know that. The duties of your congregational servant require that he spend a considerable period of his time at the points of congregational tension. He always stands in the middle! Sometime he must stand between parents and children, both of whom may have conflicting expectations of his office.

That middle ground, where the crunch is worst, is his normal position. Day after day he stands between male and female, educated and unschooled, young and old, rich and poor, have and have-nots, white and non-white, community and church. It's tough. Tension is a fact of his vocational life! Almost anything he does, or says, is going to irritate someone as much as it may please others. He better have an inner strength or, caught in this vise, he will be crushed. Praise God that in Christ Jesus he can find power to stand.

Even so, you who lead the parish ought clearly understand that this very human being never escapes far from tension. It follows him. He is not made of steel. He is as susceptible to the price that tension exacts as any other. Do not think it strange that so many pastors die young, or that they are physically afflicted with the by-product of tension. Tension (and the price it demands) is as much a ministerial vocational hazard as black-lung disease is to the miner, or the bends is to the deep-sea diver. Some things cannot be escaped. But they *can* be dealt with more effectively.

Such help will require the understanding of some, and the commitment of many. It's worth the effort. Strengthening your pastor for more effective service is the best investment of time a church council can make. And, please don't say, "I face tension, too!" As one who stands in the two worlds represented in your church council, the circumstances aren't the same.

The pain is as intense, but the options for finding relief differ markedly! A myriad of factors leave him with few of the choices you have. He can use your understanding and help. Open your eyes and reach out your hand.

5. **Pastors need help in coping with change.**

The changes that concern me are not just the changes in the world around us, but the useful change that takes place within us. A *Study of Generations* suggests that as people get older they change. Pastors get older—and they change, too. However, sometimes a younger pastor has so convinced a congregation of a given course that when he gets older, and sees other alternatives, the congregation won't allow any change to take place.

In addition many of us feel that change really only takes place by watering down some kind of eternal value. The option of change becomes, for that person, a sign of weakness. That's not so. There's an ancient Latin observation that reminds us, "The times are changing and we are changing in them." If that's not modern enough I would share with you the words of a fine old fellow from North Carolina. He told me, "A rut is really only a grave—with the ends kicked out."

Churches need to accept the value of change. Constitutions ought be regularly reviewed with change in mind. Practices should always be up for reconsideration and change. Attitudes constantly need re-evaluation and change. And the style of ministry which a pastor lives out ought be permitted to change. More than that, it ought be encouraged to do so. Oh, no, we don't seek change with regard to basic thrusts, or foundation conviction. Not that! But long before you get to that point great areas of useful change can be considered.

I'm convinced many pastors leave congregations, prematurely, because they feel it's time for a change in the parish and they aren't sure the people will let change take place. At least not while they are pastor. Or, they are afraid they won't be able to cope with the change which the congregation needs and for that reason let themselves be led elsewhere. A little healthy conversation on the subject of change won't hurt a thing. It can only help.

Remember, Lutheran Christians believe that change is not only possible, but desirable. That's what conversion, regeneration and sanctification are all about. Expand your horizons on the subject of change. Your pastor needs the wisdom you have gained. He needs it whether he's fresh out of the seminary, or knocking on the door of retirement. You have more experience in this than he. A Lutheran layman learns early in his Christian life that he must be open to the changes which each new pastor, or membership in each different congregation, brings.

Let's Talk About It

A number of concerned Christians have been doing studies about the clergy for some years. One conclusion is that there is a marked difference between the expectations of the laity toward the office of the ministry, and the expectation of the professional church worker toward his office. To illustrate this, and perhaps trigger a discussion, list the three most important things you think a professional church worker (your pastor, or teacher) does. Share your list with the other members of the church council. How much agreement to you have? Now try them out on the pastor.

As church councilmen, you ought to know what the pastor basically does with his time. List the three things you think he spends most of his time doing. Now let the pastor react to those items in as factual way as he can.

As another little exercise, read aloud his call documents, and the accompanying letter your congregation sent him expressing your expectations of him. Go through these documents with him section-by-section. What's the relationship between what you asked him to do and what he is presently doing?

If you have other full-time servants in your congregational service have the same kind of conversation with them. Specifically, try to isolate, in writing, areas in which you expect change for the good of your servants, and just as precisely spell out areas in which you seek change in the congregational expectation and use of the pastoral office. Then, as leaders in the church, make those changes happen. You can. In reality, you're probably the only group who can.

9

The End
of the Beginning?

Here we are. We're temporarily about out of pages and the words to fill them. But where are we?

Some who have gotten this far may think they've reached the end. But this is no concluding chapter bent on wrapping everything up in a tidy bundle. Those who are looking for that kind of conclusion are bound to be unhappy.

Some others are already well ahead of this point where we leave off. They've been on the journey to improved effectiveness for such a long time that most of what we've done together is what they have long wanted to do—or long ago started. Already they are casting around for the proper point of departure for the next leg of the journey. Go with God! I'm sure we'll meet again somewhere down the road.

Still others, not quite as well organized, are at a distinct point which might best be called the-end-of-the-beginning. It's now time for them to launch out on their own in exploration of those fascinating byways noted enroute to this point. Go ahead! Venture with Christ! Nothing can match that attitude toward life for the exhilaration, excitement, and ultimate joy it guarantees.

Can we pause a moment to think of those who never got this far? Maybe next time they'll make it. As you meet those who started, and then gave up, be kind to them. Pray for them. Give them a hand. We know there's so little time—and so much to do.

As we part company for now I commend you to the grace and mercy of the Lord. May the blessings of our almighty God, Father, Son and Holy Ghost be with you now and forever.

And one concluding thought. I don't believe that any one of us is as smart as all of us. Would you be kind enough to share with me your experiences, your new discoveries, your vision? I assure you I'll happily share it with others. I'd love to hear from you.

Now it's time to go about writing the history which a later *Study of Generations* will investigate and evaluate. Write with clarity so that all may see, and rejoice in, the great things God has done in this, our generation.